To our favorite little humans: Felix, Lulu, and Coco —MB, MS, and ST

To Dénes and Mosi—let me introduce you to an old friend of mine.... —MO

About This Book

The illustrations for this book were done using pencil sketches on paper and digital coloring techniques. This book was edited by Samantha Gentry and designed by Karina Granda. The production was supervised by Bernadette Flinn, and the production editor was Jen Graham. The text was set in Brandon Text, and the display type is KG Tangled Up In You 2.

Little, Brown and Company
Hachette Book Group
1290 Avenue of the Americas, New York, NY 10104
Visit us at LBYR.com

First Edition: March 2022

Little, Brown and Company is a division of Hachette Book Group, Inc.
The Little, Brown name and logo are trademarks of Hachette Book Group, Inc.

The publisher is not responsible for websites (or their content) that are not owned by the publisher.

Library of Congress Cataloging-in-Publication Data
Names: Bloom, Molly Hunegs, 1983– author. | Sanchez, Marc, 1970– author. | Totten, Sanden, author. | Orodán, Mike, illustrator.
Title: Brains on! presents...Earth friend forever / by Molly Bloom, Marc Sanchez, and Sanden Totten ; illustrated by Mike Orodán.
Other titles: Earth friend forever
Description: First edition. | New York, NY : Little, Brown and Company, 2022. | Audience: Ages 8–12. | Summary:
"A fun and informative picture book, structured as a letter from Earth to the reader about the destruction plastic is
having on the planet and how readers can help by recycling and going green!" —Provided by publisher.
Identifiers: LCCN 2020040856 | ISBN 9780316459419
Subjects: LCSH: Environmental protection—Juvenile literature. | Conservation of natural resources—Juvenile literature. | Nature conservation. |
Plastics—Recycling—Juvenile literature. | Recycled products—Juvenile literature. | Earth—Juvenile literature.
Classification: LCC TD170.15 .B56 2022 | DDC 363.7—dc23
LC record available at https://lccn.loc.gov/2020040856

ISBN 978-0-316-45941-9

PRINTED IN CHINA

APS

10 9 8 7 6 5 4 3 2 1

brains on! PRESENTS...

EARTH FRIEND FOREVER

MOLLY BLOOM, MARC SANCHEZ, and SANDEN TOTTEN

Illustrated by **MIKE ORODÁN**

L B

Little, Brown and Company

New York   Boston

Dear little humans living on me:
It's your E.F.F.!*

*Earth Friend Forever

We're old pals, right? I remember when you were just a new baby species, learning to walk upright. So cute.

Now look at you! You've walked on the moon!
(Moon says it tickled.)

And hey, you know
I've always been here
for you. I make waves—
you surf them!

I grow fruits and vegetables—
you turn them into pizza!
(Which I would *totally*
eat if I could.)

And of course I make plenty of fresh air for you to breathe.

I always have your back because you live on mine.

But there's something we need to talk about.

You're covering me
with plastic!

Like the other day I was admiring my oceans, and what did I find? So much plastic! In fact, every year, over eight million tons end up there!

That's like a garbage truck full of plastic dumped into the water *every minute*! Ick!

And it's not just my oceans. There's plastic in my forests,

on my mountains,

and in my deserts.

IT'S
EVERYWHERE!

Look, I get it. Plastic is pretty amazing stuff. It's super lightweight, you can form it into almost any shape or size, and it's really strong.

I've watched you use it to make devices that save lives, cars that pollute less, and computers where you can share pictures of me and Moon.

Your creativity blows my mind!

We've had some pretty cool adventures thanks to plastic too.
In fact, you've made it look really fun to live on me!

But here's the thing:
It turns out plastic doesn't go away. You can put it
in the garbage and it will go to a landfill.

But then it just sits there. Buried forever.
And it's really itchy! Am I getting a rash?

It's making the animals
uncomfortable too.

Some have tried eating it. Others have gotten tangled up in it.
All of them are sick of it.

You see, plastic isn't like wood or metal or banana peels. My little bacteria buddies are great at eating those things, so they break down and become part of nature again.
Nice work, bacteria!

Sadly, they're not so great at eating plastic.

So the plastic piles just
grow and **grow**.

I'm worried that one day I'll be nothing *but* plastic!

But I know you won't
let that happen. We're
best friends. Plus, you've
got those super brains.
I know you can solve
this problem.

For starters, you can recycle some plastic
and use it again. Hold your hand up.
Did you feel that breeze?

That's me high-fiving you
for recycling.

You can also replace plastic things with cloth, glass, or metal.

Every time I see you refill a water bottle instead of buying a plastic one, it makes me spin with joy.

I'm a huge fan of
canvas tote bags too,

and Moon likes seeing you use
metal straws instead of plastic
ones you throw away.

So how about it?

Can we make a planet pact to use less pesky plastic?

Oh, and when you're exploring me with your family,
you can pick up plastic and recycle it or put it in the trash.
Ah, it feels good to be clean!

In fact, why not join a beach cleanup with your friends?
Beach hangs are the best! And they show me you really care.
Can you tell that this globe is glowing?

Someday you could even become one of the scientists who are inventing new ways to recycle and break down plastic so it's not sitting in landfills forever.

Seriously, scientists are my heroes!

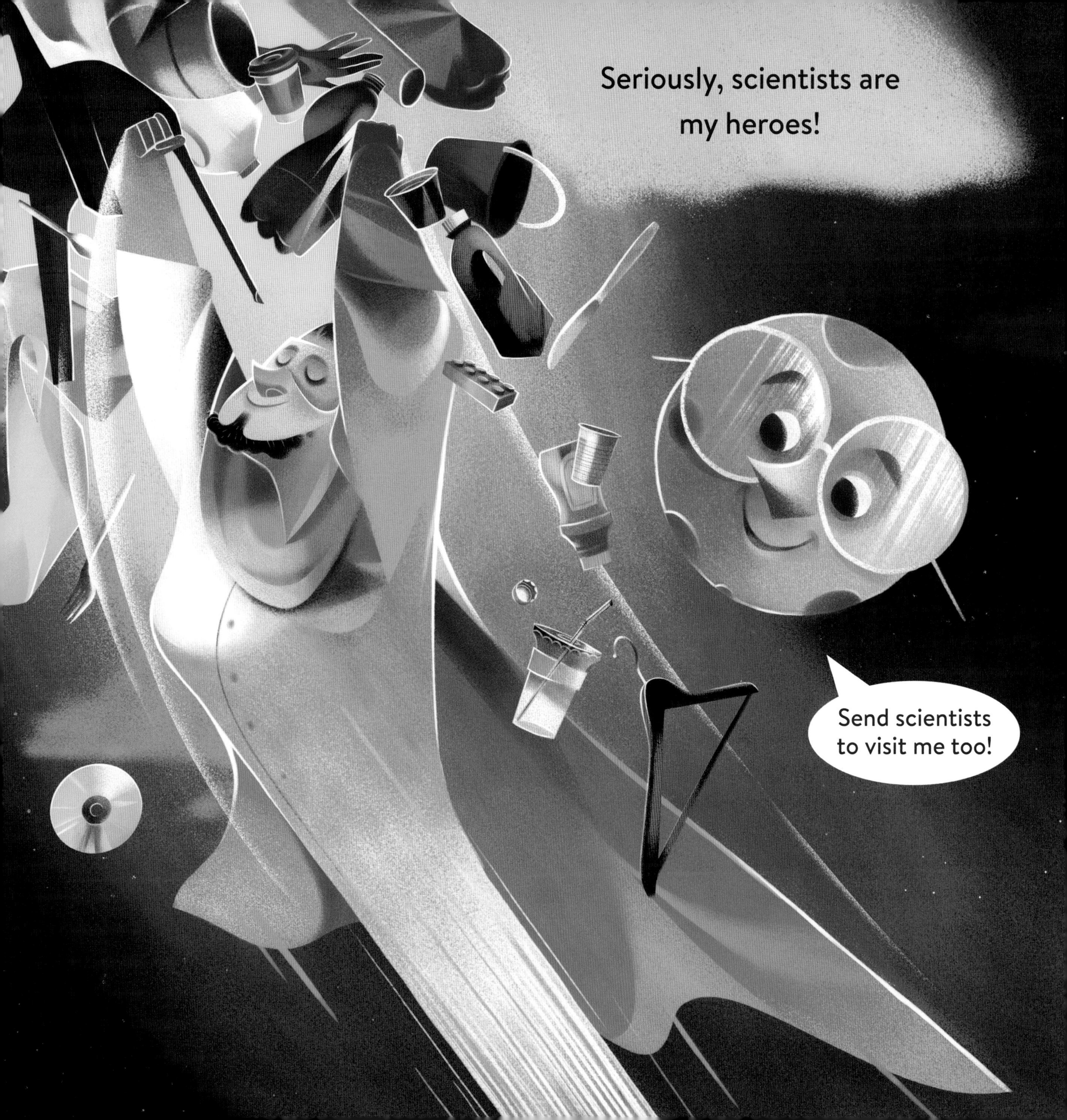

Well, little humans,
I'm glad we had this talk. I feel
better knowing you're going to
help me out. I can always count
on you to have my back.
After all, you live on it.

Love,
Your E.F.F.

Dear Earth,

You really are the best pal we could ever ask for. You give us air to breathe, food to eat, water to drink, and more beauty than one brain can handle. Sunsets? Falling snow? Butterfly wings? Melted cheese on a pizza? Breathtakingly gorgeous, each and every one.

So we just want you to know we're going to do everything we can to protect you. We're going to start thinking about the plastic in our lives—figuring out how we can use less of it, recycling what we do use, and making sure the stuff we can't recycle ends up in the trash and not the ocean. We'll pick up litter when we see it and tell our friends to do it too!

We've got your back, Earth. Thanks for letting us live on it.

Your friends forever,
Us

WHAT IS PLASTIC?

Plastics are polymers, which is a way to describe what they're made of. If you zoom way, way in, you'd see what looks like a bunch of different chains. All the chains swirl in different directions and stick together in some places. Think of a bird's nest or a plate of spaghetti. The chains are where polymers get their name. *Poly = many*, and *mers = units*. Many units!

HOW IS PLASTIC MADE?

Some plastics are made by the natural world—like rubber, which comes from plants, or silk, which comes from insects. But what we know today as plastic is synthetic, which means it's made by humans. There are a lot of different kinds of plastics, and they're not all made in exactly the same way. But here are the basics: Crude oil and natural gas are broken down into tiny molecules, which turn into the small chainlike things we mentioned earlier—polymers. Those polymers are then melted and mixed with all kinds of additives and colors, making resin. The resin cools and gets chopped into pellets, which are sent to factories where they are again melted and molded and pulled into all kinds of shapes, from straws to lawn chairs to polyester thread.

FAST FACTS

- Only about 9 percent of plastic actually gets recycled.

- Many governments are passing laws to help reduce plastic waste, like bans on plastic shopping bags or straws. This is a good start, and we'll need more cooperation and action from our leaders and businesses to solve this problem.

- Microplastics are minuscule bits of plastic that come from clothes, or bigger plastic that has broken down into tiny pieces. Scientists have found a lot of these microplastics in the ocean.

- In 2018, scientists created an enzyme that can break down plastic, and in 2020, scientists discovered a strain of bacteria that can do the same. Some fungi have also been able to break down plastic.

- Light, strong, and flexible plastic has done good for the world too: Plastic has made medicine cleaner and safer; it's made many lifesaving medical devices possible; it makes airplanes and cars lighter, so they go farther on less fuel; and it's what our computers, phones, and tablets are made of!

SCIENCE SOLUTIONS IN THE WORKS

- Developing ways that make sure plastic is disposed of properly

- Inventing systems to recycle more kinds of plastics

- Creating plastics out of biodegradable materials

- Changing the materials goods are packaged in

- Cleaning up the plastic in the ocean